MAKE THE CHOICES <u>NOW</u> TO GIVE YOURSELF THE FUTURE YOU WANT!

"What, I ask you, could be more rightly thrilling than seeing yourself change right in front of your own eyes? Not a superficial, temporary change, but a permanent, fundamental change in the kind of person you are! If your heart has yearned for a practical, powerful guide which cuts right through the nonsense and which, in plain language, goes straight to the heart of what to do to start being a new and higher *you*, this book has everything you need to get you started—*today!*"
— **Dr. Stephen Hamby, Ph.D.**

"Some of the most powerful reading I have experienced. The ideas and exercises are extremely self changing. I am amazed at the glimpses of mental clarity I have experienced."
— **Marc Whitman, AIA**

"In this book you'll be given the secret keys that put you in command of your life journey and all of its experiences. You will learn how to design your own destiny. There are such secrets. They are real. They can be yours!"
— **Ken Roberts**
author of *A Rich Man's Secret*

ABOUT THE AUTHOR

Guy Finley has enjoyed numerous successful careers, including composing award-winning music for many popular recording artists, motion pictures, and television programs. From 1970 through 1979, he wrote and recorded his own albums for the prestigious Motown and RCA record labels. Guy is the son of late-night talk show pioneer and radio celebrity Larry Finley.

In 1980, after travels to India and parts of the Far East in search of Truth and Higher Wisdom, Guy voluntarily retired from his flourishing career in order to simplify his life and continue with his inner studies.

DESIGNING
YOUR
OWN
DESTINY

THE POWER
TO SHAPE
YOUR FUTURE

By Guy Finley
Foreword By Ken Roberts
Introduction By Dr. Charles Stephen Hamby

1995
Llewellyn Publications
St. Paul, Minnesota 55164-0383, U.S.A.

Second Printing, 1995

Cover art and design: Thomas Grewe
Inside design and layout: W design
Editor: Rosemary Wallner
Project Coordinator: Pamela Henkel

Cataloging-in-Publication Data
Designing your own destiny : the power to shape your
future / Guy Finley.
    p. cm. — (Llewellyn's strategies for success series)
    ISBN 1-56718-278-X
    1. Success—Psychological aspects. 2. Self-efficacy.
3. Self-actualization (psychology). I. Title. II. Series.
    BF637.S8F55 1995
158'.1—dc20   95-30794
                                             CIP

Llewellyn Publications
A Division of Llewellyn Worldwide, Ltd.
P.O. Box 64383, St. Paul, MN 55164-0383

To Write to the Author

If you wish to contact the author or would like more information about this book, please write to the author in care of Llewellyn Worldwide, and we will forward your request. Both the author and publisher appreciate hearing from you and learning of your enjoyment of this book. Llewellyn Worldwide cannot guarantee that every letter written to the author will be answered, but all will be forwarded. Please write to:

Guy Finley
c/o Llewellyn Worldwide
P.O. Box 64383-K278-X,
St. Paul, MN 55164-0383, USA

Please enclose a self-addressed stamped envelope for reply, or $1.00 to cover costs. If outside U.S.A., enclose international postal reply coupon.

Free Catalog From Llewellyn Worldwide

For more than 90 years, Llewellyn has brought its readers knowledge in the fields of metaphysics and human potential. Learn about the newest books in spiritual guidance, natural healing, astrology, occult philosophy, and more. Enjoy book reviews, new age articles, a calendar of events, plus current advertised products and services. To get your free copy of *Llewellyn's New Worlds of Mind and Spirit*, send your name and address to:

Llewellyn's New Worlds of Mind and Spirit
P.O. Box 64383-K278-X,
St. Paul, MN 55164-0383, USA

A SPECIAL NOTE FROM THE AUTHOR

Designing Your Own Destiny was originally published as *The Key of Kings* under a special licensing agreement with 4 Star Books, a division of the Ken Roberts Company. The first edition of *The Key of Kings* was published in November 1993. *Designing Your Own Destiny* is a revised and expanded version of *The Key of Kings*.

CONTENTS

PART THREE:
SUCCESS THROUGH HIGHER SELF-STUDIES

A WELCOMING FOREWORD
FROM
KEN ROBERTS

Great men are they who see that the spiritual is stronger than material force, that thoughts rule the world.

—Ralph Waldo Emerson

Why did you pick up this book?

Could it be that somewhere in your heart you long to understand Emerson's statement? That within you is that uncommon wish to dwell in the undisturbed depths of your own True Nature, above the tempests of a world filled with heartache and confusion?

If your answer is "yes," and I trust that it is, maybe you'd like to know what's next.

Maybe you've been wondering what *you* can do to awaken that Great Power that is the foundation of inner health, wealth, and peace.

You can start by preparing yourself for a series of powerful and life-changing self-discoveries! For this book you're holding is actually a special kind of bridge that will deliver you to the real answers—and strengths you've been seeking. Here at last is a book that teaches, *directly*, what you can do to find what is genuinely life-changing. In a way, you now stand at that same intersection where Robert Frost once found himself, and later wrote of, in his timeless verse about personal choice:

> *Two roads diverged in a wood, and I*
> *I took the one less traveled by,*
> *And that has made all the difference.*
> —The Road Not Taken

These pages written by Guy Finley comprise a very unique guidebook for the sincere seeker of the Higher Life. It can lead you through that elusive transition from *working with* helpful ideas *to the actual discovery*—the *experience*—of a Higher World within you.

You'll gain conscious access to that interior part of your own psyche where your actual life-experience is being created from one moment to the next. Yes, this book is for those who desire to *cross* that secret bridge; the one that leads directly to a powerful new awareness that fears *no* circumstance because it is in total command of *its own destiny*. Doesn't this sound just like the kind of life you've always hoped for but never dared dreamed was possible?

I assure you: Such an uncompromising life *can* be yours. All you need to succeed is some New, True Knowledge—anchored with your sincere wish to be all that your Heart of hearts is urging you to be.

At this point maybe you're asking, What kind of New Knowledge has the power to deliver me to such a fearless life?

xvi   DESIGNING YOUR OWN DESTINY

For a brief look into the bright new self-understanding that awaits you, allow me to refer you to one of Guy's earlier best-selling works, *The Secret of Letting Go* (Llewellyn, 1994). In this classic self-development book, Guy relates the little-known story of how Genghis Khan, the historically infamous Mongol warlord, defeated many of his enemies from *within* their own ranks by using psychological warfare. In fact, as amazing at it may seem, some of Khan's victories were achieved without a battle! Let's see how he accomplished this, then we'll learn how our new knowledge can help to positively transform our present situation.

Khan would send specially trained agents in advance of his own approaching army. These people would dress and pose as common peasants in order to infiltrate the enemy's camp. Once accepted as locals who were loyal and apparently belonged there, Khan's secret agents would talk to the people encamped there, spreading alarming stories about the vast size, fierceness, and invincibility of Khan's forces. Since these tales of terror appeared to be coming from their own people—who had no reason to lie—the soldiers and other camp followers accepted the stories as the truth; which meant there was no other choice in the face of such insurmountable odds. The only wise thing to do was to surrender to Khan and hope for mercy.

What do you think? Does something seem strangely familiar about this bit of history? It should; there's an ongoing story in our own psyche similar to this one. Yes, we're being deceived and misdirected daily by our present way of thinking. But the light of a new and higher understanding can free us from this deception and all its sad defeats. And this means...we *can* have a new destiny if we so choose.

If you're anything like me, and feel as I did when first coming to discover that all my defeats in life were an "inside job," maybe your wish to know more about yourself just got a little stronger. Good! That's all it takes for now. Ignore those parts of yourself telling you that trying to change your destiny with only *a wish* for a Higher Life is like trying to climb Mt. Everest with a stepladder. Instead of submitting to these inner-voices of defeat, use your energies to consider the following.

Think for just a moment about what's involved in simply tying a shoelace. Now consider the task of trying to write a comprehensive set of instructions for this relatively easy physical task. Seems overwhelming—almost an impossibility—doesn't it? And yet, five-year-olds rather quickly learn to tie their own shoelaces in spite of the odds. Why? Because they don't *think* about and dwell upon the intricacies of the job they're undertaking. They just naturally respond to their own paramount wish to be able to tie their own shoelaces. *That one wish* is all they need to realize their dream and desire. And so it is that *your* wish for a Higher Life attracts *to you* all that you need to succeed, too. In fact, you may not realize this yet, but it's that very wish that has placed this special book into your hands.

So, don't stop now! Work with Guy Finley's principles, apply the practices, study the insights, and embrace the exercises. Look upon them as though they can help you to start your whole life over again on a Higher and happier level. For they can. Do this special inner work—as outlined—*and then* you'll know:

Designing your own destiny is the greatest pleasure on earth. For once you know the secret of how to choose in favor of what is True, you also know, forever, how to choose in favor of you.

Ken Roberts is founder and CEO of a multinational financial education company

INTRODUCTION
BY
DR. CHARLES STEPHEN HAMBY

Applying the principles of most books on self-transformation is like trying to build a house with rubber nails: It's a frustrating process that just doesn't work. Best-selling author Guy Finley knows this and his latest book, *Designing Your Own Destiny*, shows it.

This book contains none of the usual confusing fluff. It is definitely not for the faint-hearted or fuzzy-headed. It is not for those looking for a softer, easier way. It is not for those who secretly hope a "lazy person's guide to cosmic consciousness" might exist after all.

No! This book is for those who are fed up with half measures, who are tired of trying to make the unworkable work. It's for those who are ready to become acquainted with the power of the unvarnished but unutterable beautiful truth that Guy Finley so masterfully spells out in his newest work. If your heart has yearned for a practical, powerful guide that cuts through the nonsense and which, in plain language, goes straight to the core of exactly what to do to make this Truth your own, this book will give you everything you need to get started today.

As I hope you can tell, work is required. Yes, it can be difficult, but it is always fascinating at the same time. Work for what? For rewards that are literally "Out of this World."

What, I ask you, could be more profoundly and rightly thrilling than to see yourself change in front of your very eyes? Not a superficial, temporary change but a permanent and fundamental change in the type of person you are. Believe me, once you have glimpsed that this is possible, there will be no stopping you.

In spiritual currency, experience is everything. Knowledge and insight are interesting and sometimes even helpful, but *nothing* can substitute for having a life-transforming experience. Not reading about one. Not thinking about one. Not talking about one. The only thing that really counts is whether or not someone becomes a new person. Guy clearly shows what someone must do—and more importantly, stop doing—to realize this prize of Self-Newness. With the help of the exacting Principles in this book, you can go as fast as you want to go, spiritually speaking; and after your first reading of this life-changing material, you'll want to go plenty fast!

In Guy's practical and inviting, step-by-step style of bringing what has always been invisible into view, he reveals, and so removes, many would-be roadblocks to inner-transformation. The reader is saved enormous amounts of time and useless frustration and is handed new, reliable methods for obtaining everything needed for real spiritual success.

Among the most inspiring discoveries revealed in *Designing Your Own Destiny* are the ones Guy includes in Exercise 8, "Erase those Fearful Feelings." He first convincingly shows that fear is always an impostor emotion; but, more importantly, he lays out precisely what to do to dis-identify from this state as it attempts to arise within us. These new insights and their practices immediately weaken the terrible hold that fear has on us.

Guy points out that seeing a fear fade is only one of the thrilling successes that await you. Before ending this exercise, he explains not only how fear is defeated, but also how the requisite courage always comes as needed, as the natural and sure result of learning how to consciously invite and receive it.

In Chapter 3, "Designing Your Own Destiny," Guy introduces another powerful method that yields swift, discernible, and long-lasting relief. And here is that one, great, spiritual capacity with the power to "make straight the crooked places in our lives":

We're shown that our natural power to *stay awake*, to remain consciously aware of ourselves, is everything; and that, in fact, this new awareness is what gives us the powers needed to design our own destiny. Vernon Howard, another of my favorite self-development authors, supports these findings when he writes: "The spiritual secret of the ages is to be aware of what you are doing at the moment you are doing it."

Guy unleashes this power of heightened self-awareness for you in his own superb formula and then helps to make its power your own when he answers many questions about this little-understood internal force. The reader is supplied with accessible answers to such concerns as:

- "What makes awareness so important?"

- "Aren't I *already* aware?"

- "What do I have to do to practice higher awareness?"

- "Is meditation the same as awareness?"

If you're anything like me and you've ever wondered whether there are straightforward answers to these and other questions of a similar vital vein, the answer is a resounding yes! And there's more!

Self-deception has been defined as standing on a scale to weigh yourself while holding your stomach in! Whether this thought is seen as humorous or not, the psychological truth hidden within it is in plain sight. All students of the spiritual life eventually come face-to-face with some form of self-deception as they walk the upward Path that leads to a new destiny. Fortunately, these twists in the road don't have to turn into an insurmountable problem, because Guy has traveled far enough along the Path himself to be able to provide the necessary guidance, which he does beautifully.

First, he shows us the vital connection between our present level of awareness and the degree of self-deception that this same level enables within us. Then, he emphasizes a point that is rarely brought up in most discussions of spiritual do's and don'ts: the importance of *not* doing what the automatic self seems to require. He shows over and over how *not* going along with our unconscious habitual thoughts and identifying with terrorizing emotions releases us to perceive and receive what is True: a revelation of new inner strength waiting there all along. And then he gently reminds us again that everything needed for our success is available *now*.

When Guy takes aim at dispelling the power of the false personality in order to make room within us for what is real, he pulls everything together for the reader. He shows that even though seeing through this false nature is difficult at first, it can be done; for after all, this false nature *is* false.

He shows us in many sparkling examples that intelligence and strength are not required resources for causing our self-defeating self to disappear. Instead, we're gently shown that a preference for the sometimes unsettling truth about ourselves, to comforting but treacherous lies, is the needed commodity. And should we temporarily lack this royal resource, we're further encouraged *and assured* that even our simple *desire* to be able to embrace what is True will start us on our Way to that New and Higher Life we seek. We soon find out, of course, that the Truth we may have once feared is our friend after all. It's a fine day when, after much work in self-facing, you begin to sense the first effects of the gradual but definite and permanent fading away of the false self.

After reading this book, you'll see that there is nothing mysterious about success in spiritual matters. All crushing defeats and crippling weaknesses can be overcome. Despite all obstacles, the Truth can be known and won...for and by *you*. There is, in fact, nothing too difficult for you to accomplish. You can be perfectly equal to every task that you set for yourself or that this world delivers to your door. You *can* win. Follow Guy's friendly and inspiring instructions and make up your mind right now to go all the way. Let nothing stop you. You can change your life.

As Guy Finley says, "The future isn't a time to come, it's a choice you make right now." So dare to make that choice in favor of yourself and dare make it irrevocable. Trust your noblest impulses, and follow them into what I know will be a bright tomorrow.

Begin your journey now.

Dr. Charles Stephen Hamby, Ph.D., is a practicing clinical psychologist and a Fellow of the American Academy of Psychologists Treating Addiction.

PART ONE

GETTING STARTED

CHAPTER 1

Why You Should Feel Encouraged

L earning how to design your own destiny is not like learning to repair a clock or master a new language. So it's important to realize—right here at the outset—that if it takes time to develop and perfect even such common skills as these, how much more so is asked of those of us who would learn how to shape our own future!

That's why you must be patient with yourself. And I assure you with this brand new study material you're about to read, your patience will be rewarded.

In the pages that follow, you'll encounter some ideas and insights that you've probably never considered before. In fact, I'm sure you haven't. The Keys in this book are to inner doors that few have suspected existed—let alone thought to open and enter. But you can succeed. In fact, you may not know it yet, but you've already taken your first steps toward something Higher.

How?

Just by having this material in your hands, your destiny is already new and different. I'll explain.

That part of yourself that led you to acquire this book already belongs to an existing Higher Line of Destiny within you. That's correct. The wish itself—to be a Higher person—comes to you from a Higher place and is received in its inner equivalent within you. This means there's already an existing connection between the you that you want to be and the you that you presently are; between the new destiny you would have, and the fortunes you've known. All you have to do is stay on the Royal Road that has brought you up to this very point, for it leads directly to that Higher Destiny you seek. And now you're about to begin another leg of your appointed journey.

There's so much ahead of you that's new and exciting. But you must remember that the best views are always the higher ones, whose new heights take personal effort to achieve. To ensure you'll make steady progress along this Higher Way, allow me to instruct and encourage you in two special ways.

First: as you proceed with these new life lessons about winning the Higher Life, you may come to certain moments where you have a disquieting feeling that you don't understand what you're doing or, for that matter, *even why you're doing it!* But each time you get ready to throw your hands up in the air or toss in the towel, do your best to remember the following. For as strange as this may seem to you as you stand there, feeling oh-so uncertain, here's the true perspective to be embraced: These are the *good times*, not the bad ones! In fact, all along you've been work-ing toward just these moments.

How can this be possible? Permit me to explain.

Your confusion indicates that you have reached a real inner threshold; you stand be-fore the possibility of entering into something genuinely new *to you*. And this unthinkable place is the same as the doorway to a new destiny. So take heart!

Second, if you'll simply persist with your journey, you'll pass right through these times of trial. I guarantee it. Nothing can stop your sincere inquiry, including those thoughts and feelings telling you that you can't go any fur-ther because you don't understand how to take the next step. *Take that step anyway. Then* you'll understand.

The Light from one small moment of honest self-inquiry is more powerful than the accumulated darkness of a million years of doubt. So dare to proceed…and succeed!

SPECIAL SUMMARY

All uncertainty is Life's special invitation to enter the mystery of the ever-new—and once within this timeless world to discover yourself there as its keeper.

CHAPTER 2

A Special Invitation
to be One of the Few

For as long as men and women have walked this earth, they've been unlocking the mysteries of the world around them. It is our nature to delve, discover, and push the limits of the known. One by one, from fire to fusion, we have patiently but persistently coerced Mother Nature's great secrets out into the open and into our service.

But for all our insights and conquests over the forces of life around us, we are still living very much in the dark when it comes to understanding the nature of those forces that dwell *within* us.

What about this uncharted world within? What do we really know of its oceans of surging emotions? Of its countless invisible forms of thought? And yet, when put to question, few are troubled to admit it's these same unseen forces at work in this inner world that actually determine the way in which our outer one turns. Which makes the following all the harder to understand: Why does this essential world, which exists in the very heart of us, go unsought and so superficially examined?

With so much to gain, with so many powers to be uncovered like layers of treasure in a sunken chest, why are there so few who will dare to probe—and so possess—all the breathtaking and self-empowering secrets of their own innermost self?

This book is your invitation to be one of the few. In your hands are all the instructions you need to make the journey to this invisible world within and, upon your safe arrival, to take possession and command of your own thoughts and feelings. What an adventure awaits you once you gain the powers needed to design your own destiny.

In our travels and studies together, we're going to find out why so much of our daily direction seems to come out of default. Why does it seem that when we really want to do—or to be—something truly new and different, we almost always wind up doing just the opposite; where instead of meeting the greater challenge, we find ourselves taking the path of least resistance, and then either blaming someone or something for our condition; or else sadly resenting ourselves for our own weakness. Instead of meeting the greater challenge, we find ourselves taking the path of least resistance. We blame either someone or something for our condition or sadly re-sent ourselves for our own weakness.

If you've had enough of being too much for yourself, *Designing Your Own Destiny* holds all the tools you need to discover, and then call upon, a new Source of Strength that will make you the ruler of your own life. In this book, you'll be given the secret keys that put you in command of your life journey, as well as all its experiences. You will learn how to determine your own destiny. There are such secrets. They are real. And they can be yours.

In the eleven powerful inner-life exercises that are the heart and body of this book, you'll discover how to become conscious of, and completely master, both the strong and subtle forces that determine your life-choices. And since it is these life-choices, *your daily decisions*, which ultimately decide your direction in life, becoming conscious of the invisible inner influences that determine these decisions will be the same as taking into your hands the reins of your own destiny.

Repeat: You can learn how to be that rarest of individuals who is always going exactly where he or she wants to be going; one whose entire life experience—each and every step along the chosen way—never fails to be self-enriching. This is the life that's intended to be your destiny! Let's gather the facts that will deliver its realization.

SPECIAL SUMMARY

To go beyond yourself, you must first *be* yourself. To be yourself takes no special understanding, only a willingness to *see* yourself as you really are.

CHAPTER 3

Designing Your Own Destiny

It is a Law not of man's or woman's but of Life: Before you can have a different life; before you can be happier, wiser, more at peace, and in quiet command of yourself, you must first be different. *Being* is everything.

WHAT IS BEING?

A moment's consideration helps determine that everything around us has some form of Being. Why is this true? Because all physical forms—whether animated or not—are expressions of that One Great Life whose vast intelligent and creative energies are the foundation of all we perceive. So we can reason

15

that even a common rock has Being of a sort. Similarly, all manner of Beings—from rocks to roses to you and I (all unique expressions of this One Great Energy)—possess a *nature*.

WHAT GIVES SOMETHING ITS NATURE?

The nature of a rock is determined entirely by the natural forces acting upon it. This means its Being is without any choice; which further means that both the rock's nature—and its destiny—are, in fact, predetermined. One day it will be dust. The gradual disintegration is part of the nature of all things physical.

And neither does the rose, dressed so delicately in its fragrant velveteen petals, have a choice as to its nature. An individual rose can't choose not to have thorns or attract bees. Like the rock next to which it grows, the nature of any rose is a *fixed* expression of its Being.

But Human nature—*your* nature—*is not fixed.* It can be transformed.

This amazing quality, the inherent potential mutability of our nature, is what sets us above all God's countless other creations. And this fact about our unique nature also empowers us in a very special way. As a feature of our Being, each of us is created with the power to choose the course of our own destiny. Let's see how this is possible.

Your Being is in a constant process of unfolding. That it will unfold is not your choice. Being is a gift that came with birth. It *is*. And while Being is both the creator and cosmic animator of your individual story, how your life unfolds—the direction it takes—is something you *can* influence. It's called making choices. And being empowered to have a real voice in your life-choices is what this book is all about. See if the following makes perfect sense:

Before you can change the course of and learn to design your own destiny, you must first gain access to that secret place within yourself where your own future is being created moment by moment by moment. Yes, there is such a location. It's Real. And yes, you can learn to dwell there and direct your destiny.

This truly timeless place, where all your life-choices are made for you, is what we understand, in concept, as the Present Moment. But this state of True Now is not just an idea. It's a place of extraordinary and measureless power, for the True Present Moment is actually a Cosmic Seed of a sort, from out of which springs all that comes later. And this point brings us to one of our key lessons.

Coupled with the new knowledge you've already gained from this study, your close consideration of the following insight will bring you one step closer to taking command of your own destiny. The Present Moment is where our Being, which is a timeless unconditioned energy, meets and animates our nature. Now our nature, on the other hand, lives only in time; meaning it's fabricated from all our past experiences. Said slightly differently, our nature is a psychological body of memories and knowledge structured by our social, economic, and religious conditioning.

The Present Moment, where our being and our nature meet, *is the instant of our destiny*. And up until now, we've had little real choice in how our fates unfold because it's always been our nature—our accumulated past with all of its fears, compulsions, and doubts—that has been running the show. Just a few more facts will help us to further understand some of the inherent problems built into this unconscious inner condition.

Our present nature is a *thought nature*. It must *think* to know itself. And because the only way it can know itself is through thought, this mental nature is unable to see that many of its own thoughts are not what it thinks them to be. For instance, we've all known a certain thought that told us we were strong or that our life was "really together." But later we found ourselves badly shocked at the depth of our own self-deception. Reality came along, as it always does, and made us see that our image of ourselves was just that: only a thought with no real strength at all!

Repetitive experiences such as these should make it clear enough. Our present nature can't know when it's reached a bad decision because in that moment—as it's busy deciding our destiny using its own confused or misguided understanding—our nature is, itself, that bad choice. Not only can't it see the forest for the trees, sometimes this nature doesn't even know it's lost in the woods!

Things would be bleak indeed if there were no other choice but to live out the remainder of our lives under the conditions imposed by this limited consciousness. Our day-to-day life-situation wouldn't be too dissimilar from that of being a passenger in a coach drawn by six powerful horses with no driver to steer it! Yes, we would, no doubt, be able to get from one place to the next. But for the whole ride we would be nervous and uncertain not only about where we were headed, but also if we would arrive there at all! Sound familiar? I know it does! And our agreement serves to take us on to the next step in our journey. Perhaps the most pivotal one.

The time has come to introduce a third character to the horse and carriage metaphor. You're about to be introduced to a force in your own consciousness that, when brought to bear in each and every moment of meeting between your nature and your Being, produces both the missing driver and the reins you need to be able to begin designing your own destiny.

You can think of this third force that can be at your command as a kind of special window into the Present Moment. It's called *Awareness*. And it is the most unique feature of your nature for the following reason: Your awareness of the Present Moment *is* the Present Moment.

You can, and should, pause here for a moment to breathe some life into this last very important idea. To take it out of the realm of thought and into your direct experience, just choose to become fully aware of yourself.

If you've never tried this before, following are some helpful guidelines.

Come wide awake to your total environment *this moment*. Just know, without thinking what are all the sounds, sights, feelings, thoughts, impressions, textures, and temperatures around and within you *right now*. Again, this knowing yourself and your surroundings is not arrived at by going into thought. And if you practice this higher kind of self-presence, you'll see that *this special awareness of yourself is the same as the Present Moment in which you just became aware.* They are one and the same. Which means this self-awareness, as it includes the Present Moment, *is also a feature of your Being.* This is the inner realization we've been working toward all along.

Your awareness of the Present Moment, which is a secret part of your True Being, doesn't have to think about which direction is best for you. It knows because *it sees.* Where your usual nature is often blinded by its own unseen self-interests, your Being, represented in the moment by your awareness of it, effortlessly sees into—and through—this unconsciously compromised thinking even as it's occurring.

The presence of this Higher Intelligence keeps you from defeating yourself. And this is the same as making you newly victorious! For each time you have the awareness not to choose from that bank of old patterns produced by your limited thought nature, new and higher alternatives appear before your inner eyes. These moments, and their messages, rise to greet you from your True Being. And with these directions as your guide, designing your own destiny is as effortless as you are now confident—for how can you *not* succeed when Reality itself points your way!

SPECIAL COMMENT

For extra important benefits, please read the above section over at least once again, or until you know you're beginning to understand the new concepts it presents. It goes without saying that some of the special insights offered in this and following sections of the book can be challenging; but it *needs* to be said that these discoveries are not beyond your reach *if* you'll risk the temporary discomfort of stretching for something that seems to exceed your present grasp. But *all* is closer than you think! Here's why this is true.

The ideas in this book are based *in reality*, which is the same as saying they're accessible to *anyone who* wills *to see them*. Stated slightly differently, your success with these ideas all depends upon the strength of your wish to see beyond what your present understanding says it's possible for you to see. But when you can also see that your present level of understanding *can't know* there is something real beyond *it*, then you know what must be done to win that new and higher understanding.

So dare to reach beyond yourself—and hold that wish out there—until the new ground you would stand upon rises up beneath you. It will, if you *will*.

SPECIAL SUMMARY

The great power in true self-awareness is that nothing can come into it without its complete character being revealed upon its entrance.

CHAPTER 4

Taking the High Road that Leads to Self-Rule

Following this last, brief section, you'll be introduced to eleven exercises especially created to help you master the inner-skills needed to design your own destiny. Each one has unique properties and presents stimulating interior challenges that will help you to awaken new levels of higher self-awareness. With alert practice, you'll soon possess the power to change the direction of your life—by changing your nature—as it expresses itself in the Present Moment.

For best results, read the eleven exercises all the way through, just as you would read any book from start to finish. Then return to the individual lessons by making each one the focus of your undivided study for at least a full day.

For superior results, I suggest you work with each exercise for one complete week. Take longer if you like. But regardless of your elected length of practice time, make every effort with each exercise to work with its particular inner lessons at every available opportunity...of which you're sure to find dozens in any twelve-hour period.

Start with any one of the exercises. Maybe there is one that better suits your personal situation at the moment than another. That's fine. Whichever exercise you choose to begin your inner work, it's important that you work all the way through each of the eleven.

Here is one last suggested instruction that will help your inner work progress noticeably faster:

As you finish working with one exercise and prepare to move on to the next, continue with the practice of the one you've just completed. Even though the new exercise on your list will demand most of your attention, you can remain aware of—and continue to work on—these combined studies. You'll discover that the collective effect of these exercises supports and amplifies one another in ways that help hasten higher self-discovery.

One last note: Succeed just once—with any of these unique inner-life exercises—and your life will never be the same again. All will be new for you; both for the fact of your victory over your own time nature, and for your New Knowing that now tells you…You *can* design your own destiny!

SPECIAL SUMMARY

There is no such thing as a wasted step when your final destination is self-transformation.

PART TWO

How to Design Your Own Destiny

Exercise 1

GET ONE THING DONE

SPECIAL INSIGHT

Never mind how much there may be to do; or how hard some task appears to be.

Get one thing done and then take that step again. Consciously brush aside any other concerns. Do what's in your power. *Refuse to deal with what's not.*

THE ROAD BEFORE YOU

Have you ever had this experience? You're faced with so many things that have to be done in a timely manner that it overwhelms you...*so all you do is nothing!* Well, that is, *almost* nothing. You do manage to:

33

- Worry yourself sick about how you'll get everything done.

- Eat or snack until you feel drowsy.

- Take several naps hoping to awaken inspired.

- Reorganize your papers and desk drawers as part of your plan of attack.

- Worry about all the time you've wasted making plans and reorganizing your desk.

If you're tired of finding yourself exhausted—even before you're able to start working on some line of tasks assembled before you—this exercise is custom-made for you.

The following insights and prescribed actions will lend just the help you need to succeed in handling a hundred pressing jobs; all while enjoying that inner calm and confidence that comes with knowing that you're not only doing all that can be done but you're also doing it in the best manner!

You might be familiar with that time-tested golden adage: "All is not as it appears to be." One of the hard ways we've all learned that this old saying is true is when it comes to encountering certain smiling faces. There's no doubt about it. Appearances can and often do deceive.

But we've yet to discover that this same wise advice also holds true *to the appearance of our own thoughts.* Thoughts deceive us all the time. It's true. In fact, people deceive us because we let our own ideas about that person mislead us. We see a smiling person and assume that person is friendly. But it's not just in the area of relationships that our own thoughts deceive and betray us. Which brings us to the key insight underlying this exercise.

At any given moment, regardless of appearance or emotional certainty to the contrary, it is not the demand of those already-overdue, one hundred and one tasks that have you feeling so overwhelmed and under prepared. What you're really experiencing *is the overwhelming presence of one thought.* One thought that calls itself "one hundred and one things to do." Impossible you say? Read on.

The power that this one thought has to deceive—and to ultimately freeze you in your tracks—is born partly out of its invisible alliance with anxiety-laden emotions. Here's how these two terrible tricksters team up to keep you off track and forever running for the train.

Thoughts have the power to present themselves to your mind in picture form. These thoughts are known to us and experienced as imagination. In this instance, as it concerns our study, one thought assumes the image, or mental picture, of one hundred and one tasks yet to be completed. To illustrate to you how this kind of mental picture is possible, imagine a photograph of a terribly cluttered desk. This mental picture is, in fact, *one* image with a thousand loose ends!

What happens next is that this single mental picture, consisting of multiple superimposed images, becomes animated with anxious and pressure-filled feelings. Now in your mind's eye, that picture of your impossible situation not only looks real…it *feels* that way too! But this show has just begun.

In the wink of an eye, a second thought pops up. And unbeknownst to you, it's in league with the initial imaginary scene projected by the first thought. Its task is to confirm your worst suspicions; which it does when it announces in a small, but defeated voice that sounds a lot like your own: "It's hopeless. There's just too much to do. How can I get out of this?"

CHOOSING YOUR NEW DIRECTION

The next time you "hear" this inner voice of imminent doom, listen instead to this Higher Instruction: *Never again look for a way out of any anxious condition. Look instead for a way to see through it.*

Now learn the Higher techniques that will show you how to be a self-starting individual instead of a self-stalling one.

Each time you're faced with a logjam of tasks that seem far beyond your mortal abilities to resolve in the allotted time, here's what to do. First, whittle these logs down to manageable size by writing each one out on a pad of paper. This act will also help you untangle some of your own tangled feelings about the jam you're in. For now, forget their order of importance; that will become clear later. Just get each task down on paper. Besides, your priorities can only be as clear as your thinking, so making this list helps to clarify both. Another benefit of your list is that it will keep confusion out of the picture, and confusion is to anxiety what wind is to a dust devil.

Once you have your list of tasks written down on paper, place a star next to number one on your list. Then *do it!* What does this mean? Exactly what it says!

Take number one on your list and *just get that one thing done.* Consciously refuse to entertain any other thoughts that push themselves into your mind with images of impossibility. It *is* possible to do one thing at a time. And it *is* possible to successfully complete one thing at a time, and to do that one thing to the very best of your ability.

Then…move to the next task at hand: number two. Follow the same winning procedure as you did with number one. Then do number three and so on until all is done.

YOUR HIGHER DESTINY

The main lesson here is that success only becomes impossible when you try to deal with *what isn't* in your power. Renegade parts of you want you to waste your powers dealing with them. Your misguided attention to their punishing presence gives them a life they wouldn't have without tricking you into giving them one. This means you don't need power to deal with what's been defeating you, only the Higher Understanding it takes to consciously dismiss it from your inner life. You have that power now. Start using it.

Work with this exercise. Use its instructions. Get one thing done, one at a time, all the way down your list…whatever it may be. Proceed in spite of any thoughts or feelings that would have you believe you can't. Just behind your certainty that your "list" is too much for you lies a new and conscious capability to proceed one step at a time; to accomplish one task at a time; to your satisfaction.

SPECIAL SUMMARY

The most beautiful tapestry in the world begins and ends with but *one* of a hundred thousand threads.

> *Doubt is the vestibule which all must pass before they can enter the temple of Wisdom. When we are in doubt and puzzle out the truth by our own exertions, we have gained something that will stay by us and serve us again. But, if to avoid the trouble of the search we avail ourselves of the superior information of a friend, such knowledge will not remain with us; we have not bought, but borrowed it.*
>
> —*Caleb Colton*

Exercise 2

TAKE THE CONSCIOUS RISK

SPECIAL INSIGHT

Nothing you're afraid of losing can ever be the source of your fearlessness.

THE ROAD BEFORE YOU

Has there ever been a time in your life—a period of real self-enriching growth—that wasn't connected to a risk you either willingly undertook or—to a time of inner trial where there was no other choice for you but to take a risk? Of course, there's only one answer to this question, and its one recognized as being true wherever you may ask it in the world:

The prize of greater wisdom and inner strength always goes to those who take, in one way or another, the risk.

But one note before we go any further. I am not recommending risking your resources on ridiculous "get-rich-quick" financial schemes. Nor am I recommending risking your life by trying to cheat death with some harebrained stunt. These kinds of activities aren't really risks at all, other than on a very superficial level. Yes, risks like these may give you a temporary charge, but so does sticking your finger in an electrical socket! Real self-change goes far beyond boosting self-esteem. It's a permanent inner transformation that frees you from feeling low in the first place.

This exercise is specialized instruction, a Higher Education, in how it's possible for you to find—and then willingly enter into—Conscious Risks. With what you're about to learn, you won't have to wait for an accidental or painful event to come along and prompt you into realizing a self-liberating self-change.

You'll be empowered with a secret knowledge that will actually allow you to choose these moments of self-transformation. You will have a hand in creating your own destiny and ultimate spiritual success.

Let's take a moment to briefly review what is a conscious risk. And why these kinds of risks can be such a powerful catalyst for inner change. Then we'll learn how to locate these special risks at will, including the winning actions to take when these moments of conscious risk present themselves. But first, a definition: *A conscious risk involves making a choice to do what's true, in spite of what that choice may cost you.*

One fairly common example of this uncommon kind of inner valor is refusing to go along with the destructive behavior of someone you love—even though that choice may mean he or she walks out of your life. But even here the victory is still yours. For even in the worst-case scenarios, you always discover that what you lose is *never the thing you feared losing.*

Yes, that self-destructive man or woman may be gone for good, which hurts at first. But it's not too long before you know something else is missing too. What you really lost was a part of yourself that had been a secret slave to a false image of what it means to be loving—or to the fear of finding yourself alone. And as this revelation strengthens, which it always does, you finally can see that all you really lost was a source of unconscious sorrow you'd always mistaken for being *you!* What a relief.

These discoveries deliver into your hands a personalized invitation to find what is your own free and fearless life. We can summarize our study to this point as follows:

On the other side of any conscious risk is the realization that *who you really are* has nothing to fear. But in order to make this self-liberating discovery, you must willingly face those fears, whatever they may be.

Here's some extra encouragement. The moment of real conscious risk always feels like a tunnel with no light at its other end. But each time you'll choose to enter it, that tunnel will turn into a bridge spanning the space between your past fearful life...and your new fearless one.

CHOOSING YOUR NEW DIRECTION

Following are examples of everyday events, each of which presents a unique opportunity to take a conscious risk. And, as you'll see, even the most common occurrences hide within themselves secret bridges to new self-wisdom and greater inner strength.

1. Risk Saying No

The first step toward having your own free life begins with daring to refuse the silent demands of others. Saying "yes," for fear of saying "no" is a recipe for resentment. Risk walking away from fear. Say "no."

2. Risk Leaving Empty Spaces Empty

Giving yourself empty things to do can't fill that emptiness you feel inside. So risk leaving that space empty. Allow it to fill itself, which it wants to do, with something you can't give yourself: The end of feeling empty.

3. Risk Not Defending Yourself

It's only when you consciously risk laying down your armor, shield, and sword; your quips, retorts, and criticisms that you discover *who you really are* can't be hurt. Risk letting others win.

4. Risk Appearing Stupid

Pretending to understand something that you don't, for fear of appearing stupid, only ensures that you'll remain a fearful pretender for the rest of your life. And that's stupid. Risk asking all the questions you need to ask. *That's* smart!

5. Risk Bearing Your Own Burdens

The weight of any trouble is determined by how much you fear it. But the only weight any fear can have is what *you* give to it when you try to push it away. Risk not "sharing" your burdens. Stop pushing them onto others. You'll be amazed how light they really are.

6. Risk Being Rejected

"No" is just a word; the fear of it is a prophecy self-fulfilled. Be bold! Risk asking for what you really want. Reject the fear of being rejected by daring to say "no" to the fear of no.

7. Risk Catching Yourself in the Act

Your life can't be both a show and be real. Catch yourself in the middle of some self-created drama and just drop it. Risk bringing the curtain down on yourself. Life is real only when you are.

8. Risk Taking the Lead

You can never know the true pleasure and spiritual satisfaction of having your own life until you take the risk of finding it for yourself, all by yourself. Followers fear to tread that Higher inner road called "My Own Way." Risk going out in front.

9. Risk Letting Go

You've been trying to run your own show and, so far, it's pretty much been a nightmare with entertaining intermissions! Risk letting something Higher have Its Hand at directing your life. Let your show go.

10. Risk Being No One

Everyone wants to be seen by others as being great. This makes that kind of greatness common. Be awake to what is common in your life and then risk doing the opposite. Real Greatness follows.

YOUR HIGHER DESTINY

Look for your own moments where taking a conscious risk will lead you to a liberating self-discovery. Following is a helpful hint to get you started looking in the right inner direction.

In olden days, prospectors searched for gold along riverbanks and in the exposed beds of mountain streams. Besides knowing how to look for the right geological formations, where it was likely gold nuggets lay hidden just under the sandy gravel, the best prospectors also had a special trick up their sleeve that helped shift the odds of finding gold in their favor.

As they walked along the water's edge, they placed themselves with the sun to their back and watched for a slight glint or golden flash in the sand. They knew from experience that where there were flakes of gold, there were also chunks. By following a similar approach in your search for inner gold, you can succeed in this exercise of taking conscious risks. Here's the parallel:

Watch yourself, all the time, wherever you are and whatever you may be doing. Watch for that telltale flash of resistance, anger, frustration, anxiety, or fear. Then let your heightened inner awareness lead you to the prize of self-liberation.

Since your usual reaction to any negative emotion is to avoid the condition or person you think is responsible for that feared feeling your new and higher action is to consciously go toward that flash. In other words, don't walk away from what you see as being the source of your negative state; instead, willingly walk toward it. Trembling if you have to!

Risk it! The priceless inner gold of a fearless life is waiting there just for you.

SPECIAL SUMMARY
True strength is the flower of Wisdom, but its seed is action.

What did you do today to receive your instruction?
—*Louis Pasteur*

Exercise 3

CANCEL SELF-WRECKING RESENTMENTS

SPECIAL INSIGHT

Whatever form your resentments may take, they wreck only you... *not* the one you resent.

THE ROAD BEFORE YOU

Two men stroll down a leaf-covered wood lot path on a clear, brisk autumn morning. Jeff and Mark have been friends for years. They enjoy their Saturday morning walks and talks together. Yet, something's different about Mark today. Jeff senses there's a problem. But he says nothing.

Two minutes later, Mark stops walking and turns to Jeff. His eyes are searching for a place to begin. Then, following right behind his slowly spreading smile, these words spill out: "Jeff, are all these voices that are arguing in my head bothering you too?"

A second later, they both break out laughing. The spell Mark had been under was suddenly broken. He had been the captive of a dark inner dialogue.

What's a dark inner dialogue? Just what it sounds like: a negative tug-of-war in the unseen recesses of your mind where you're the only one pulling on both ends of the rope. Still more to the point: Being in a dark inner dialogue is finding yourself losing a heated argument when there's no one else in the room with you!

What causes these dark inner dialogues? Resentment. So, here's a key thought to help you release this self-wrecking inner state: Holding onto some hurt or hatred—over what someone may have done to you in the *past*—makes you that person's slave *in the here and Now.*

If you're tired of being a slave to a painful relationship out of your past, this study and exercise in how to release resentments is sure to bring welcome relief.

For this lesson to succeed in its intended purpose, it's important to understand that resentment is a bitter pill made up of two layers. The first layer is created by our refusal to be self-ruling: Saying "yes" when we really want to say "no!" is one good example. Fawning before others for fear of their reprisal is another. Both weak actions breed resentment, because our wish to falsely accommodate compromises our natural need to be self-commanding.[1]

The second layer is resentment's "active" ingredient; the psychological component that keeps it alive and unwell. This is the dark inner dialogue. These unconscious conflicts, in dialogue form, play themselves out in our mind by painfully reenacting various scenes from our past; moments gone by in which we

[1] From *The Secret Way of Wonder* by Guy Finley (Llewellyn Publications, 1992).

either know, or sense, we were compromised by our own weakness.

And now comes another key thought.

If these inner dialogues were left to themselves as they popped into our mind, they'd be as powerless to disturb us as an echo is to change its own sound. Where we get into trouble, when resentment rules, is when we're unknowingly drawn into these scenes out of our past and find ourselves interacting with a cast of ghost players! The ensuing mental dialogue is always a desperate but futile attempt to change *what has already been said* and done so that maybe this time around we can come out a winner.

One good example of this kind of dark inner dialogue is giving someone a heated piece of your mind—when he or she is not around to hear it!

CHOOSING YOUR NEW DIRECTION

Tired of going twelve rounds in routine fight scenes that always turn out the same?

Try this exercise for the winning solution.

If you sat down on a metal bench and suddenly realized the midday sun had heated it way beyond the comfort zone, you'd stand up as quickly as you could. The same Intelligence behind this instinctive physical reaction can help you release all resentments and drop their dark inner dialogues.

Each time you catch yourself in a dark inner dialogue, *of any kind,* use your awareness of the conflict it's creating within you as a springboard to help you leap out of those scary scenes from your past into the safety of the Present Moment. Then, instead of giving yourself back over to those inner voices of conflict that are still trying to converse with you, remain aware of yourself in the Present Moment, and of their continuing beckoning presence.

No matter how many times you hear in your mind those fighting words that have always prompted you to jump into that dark dialogue, refuse to join in. *Ground yourself in your awareness of the Present Moment.*

YOUR HIGHER DESTINY

The unconscious resentment responsible for creating heated scenes from the past cannot follow you into the *Now*, which means no dark inner dialogue can tag along either. Why? Because when you're no longer a captive of your own past, you can recognize its ghost voices as the source of psychic intrusion they really are.

Remember, no dark inner dialogue can ever solve an unresolved resentment any more than one end of a snake is less the serpent.

SPECIAL SUMMARY

Learn to ask for a happy, new life by refusing to relive what's been tearing at you.

Vengeance is mine, says the Lord.
—Old Testament

Exercise 4

STEP OUT OF THE RUSH

SPECIAL INSIGHT

Even at a million miles an hour, anxious thoughts and feelings *still take you nowhere.*

THE ROAD BEFORE YOU

Before you can step out of the rush and into your own life, you must first see that while anxious, hurried feelings often lend a temporary sense of self-importance, these same racing emotions actually rob you of the power you need to be self-commanding. A brief investigation will confirm this finding.

Self-command begins with being able to choose your own direction in life. And whether you're caught in the raging current of a white-water river, or being swept along by a flood of invisible thoughts and feelings, one fact remains: Like it or not, you're going where that current goes. You have no real choices as long as you're under its influence. That's why learning to step out of the rush is the same as learning how to step into your own life.

Allow the exercise described below to show you that your Real Nature never feels the need to rush any more than an eagle would try to swim across a lake to get to the other side.

Here's the challenge: Rushing thoughts and anxious feelings are invisible to you because each time they begin to race, *you start to run with them*. And after so many years of being carried along in this psychic slipstream, you've come to believe that either you are these surging inner currents or that their power is yours. Neither case is true. You are not these waves of thought any more than a cresting tide is the entire ocean.

Author Vernon Howard offers this emphatic instruction to help strengthen our resolve to stop this mad dash to nowhere: "Slow down. Relax. Dare to deliberately defy those inner screams that demand you rush nervously around. Instead, obey another quiet voice that assures you that the casual life is the truly powerful and efficient life."

CHOOSING YOUR NEW DIRECTION

Beginning this very moment, intentionally separate yourself from any rushing inner condition by voluntarily stepping out of it. How can this be done? *Purposefully slow yourself down* by acting to consciously reduce your usual speed. Here are several suggested ways to guarantee a good start.

1. At 50 percent your normal gait, walk over to get your cup of coffee.

2. Try reaching for the phone, your glass of water or your pen at 75 percent your normal speed.

3. Drive the speed limit (at all times) but especially when late for an appointment.

One practice I find particularly profitable, at home and in business, is to pause a few seconds *before* I answer someone's question. This special conscious pause for self-awakening is invaluable because, as the old saying goes, "Only fools rush in!" Whatever the occasion may be, choose the time and place to slow down, and then practice stepping out of the rush.

YOUR HIGHER DESTINY

Here's the secret behind how this unique exercise delivers new self-command: Slowing down helps you become aware of yourself in a new and higher way by creating contrast between your usual speed through life and your now selectively slower one.

This enhanced self-awareness empowers you to step out of the rush of your own surging thoughts and feelings *by making you con-*

scious of their flooding presence within you as being *something that doesn't belong to you.* Once this is clear, then you can choose your own direction in life. Step out of the rush by slowing down. Do it Now.

SPECIAL SUMMARY

If you want to find what is Timeless, dare to live as though you have all the time in the world.

Whoever is in a hurry shows that the thing he is about is too big for him.
> —*Philip Chesterfield*

Exercise 5

REFUSE TO BE
SELF-COMPROMISING

SPECIAL INSIGHT

Refuse to compromise yourself in the present moment for the promise of a happier one to come.

THE ROAD BEFORE YOU

Your True Nature is *Now*. There is no later. This means that before we can change the unhappy endings in our life, we must learn how to drop them before they begin. And yes, this can be done. There is no other possible order; no other real correction for getting to the root of what's been wrecking our days.

The exercise described below has the power to change everything about your life for the better because it's all about changing how the troubling things in your life really begin. Your close study of these inner life lessons will reveal a hidden story. Watch how your new vision brings you new victory.

CHOOSING YOUR NEW DIRECTION

The next time a want of any kind presses into your heart or mind, ask yourself these two questions: *How do I feel about what I want?* and *How does this want make me feel now?*

For the best results, take a piece of paper and draw a line down the middle from top to bottom. At the top of the left-hand column, write the first question. At the top of the right-hand column, write the second question.

The first step is to notice the important difference between these two questions.

In the left-hand column, write down the thoughts and emotions that appear as you imagine how you're going to feel when you get the object of this new want. Perhaps you want a new job or higher position; a better relationship; a new outfit; a vacation, or maybe that car you've been dreaming about driving across country.

What are some of the feelings that accompany such long-awaited wants? I'm sure you can list your own, but some examples include:

- excitement
- a sense of well-being
- the enjoyment of imagining yourself as the envy of all your friends

After taking inventory of how you think you're going to feel in that near or distant moment, take yourself out of this world of pleasing promises. Address the question in the right-hand column that asks you how this want makes you feel in the present moment.

Don't be concerned with what you may now discover within yourself. Just observe all those thoughts and feelings secretly attending to your want. Some of the surprising answers to "How does this want make me feel now?" could include feelings such as these:

- gripping anxiety
- disturbing or distant doubts
- worrisome fears

What exactly is happening here? Why do we find these negative states?

Follow closely: The same mind that projects a pleasure-to-come is instantly, but unconsciously, pained that it may not be able to possess that pleasure that it has imagined for itself. This invisible anguish is the root of self-compromise; for now we struggle to free ourselves from this self-created sorrow by doing "whatever it takes" to realize our wants.

YOUR HIGHER DESTINY

If you work at this exercise and consciously apply its principles each time one of those familiar, haunting wants arises, you'll understand what few men and women have ever known: Each present moment is the seed of the next; and it is the actual content of each successive present moment that brings us all that we experience as our life.

Your awakening awareness to what your wants are actually giving you will help you to change what you've been asking from life. And as your life-requests change in the *now*, in *each* present moment—from being secretly punishing to increasingly perceptive ones— you'll naturally begin to free yourself from all unconscious self-compromising acts.

SPECIAL SUMMARY

You can't be divided *and* be content, so choose in favor of self-wholeness.

He who promises runs in debt.
                                    —*The Talmud*

Exercise 6

TAKE THE STEP THAT YOU'RE SURE YOU CAN'T

SPECIAL INSIGHT
Each time you take the step that you're sure you can't, you discover that the "you" who *would not* was only a *thought* that believed it *could not*.

THE ROAD BEFORE YOU
How many times have you found yourself thinking you'd like to develop a new skill or sharpen an old one? Maybe you've wanted to learn another language or play a musical instrument; further your education; or get up

out of your easy chair and do some catch-up on that correspondence you've been putting off for weeks!

But in each, or at least most, of these instances, before you can even get started, you find yourself turned back; repelled from your upcoming chosen task by an onslaught of invisible forces! Suddenly, you're surrounded by deep weariness, self-doubt, mental fog, or sometimes just plain fear.

Do you recognize any of these self-stalling inner-attackers? Would you like to be liberated from their limiting influences? Freed to pursue higher levels of your own inner development? That's what this exercise is all about: Teaching you how to take that next step each time you're sure you can't. Let's begin by covering a few basics in Higher, or esoteric, psychology.

Most of us wouldn't be too surprised to hear that our mind has a will of its own. We all know what it's like to be more or less helplessly doing something we wish we weren't! We often feel the presence of this force within, but don't understand it—or its implications.

Figuratively speaking, every cell of your whole body has a "will" of a sort. This is a well-known scientific truth. Both the mind and the body are always hard at work, at a cellular level, to keep their lives—as they know them—in what is called "homeostasis." Don't let this strange-sounding term throw you. All it means is "the tendency of any organism, simple or complex, to want to maintain within itself relatively stable conditions." The translation as it concerns this exercise: There are more parts of you *that want to stay the same* than there are ones interested in growing or achieving new heights through effort.

The good news is that who you really are is greater than any one of these invisible aspects of yourself that are mechanically compelled to maintain its status quo. Your True Nature is greater than the sum of all these physical, mental, and emotional parts. If you have any doubts about this, it's in your power to make this Truth self-evident.

CHOOSING YOUR NEW DIRECTION

The next time you want to go ahead with any project—whether it's designing a rocket ship or finally getting around to repairing your favorite rocking chair—and you start to feel those old familiar doubts, dreads, or doldrums rising up to block your way, just *walk right through them*. You can do it if you use your new Wisdom to clear the way.

One excellent way to break through these seemingly impassable inner states is to see them as being the fakes they are. This isn't to say you won't feel their punishing presence when you first dare to defy their threats. But each time you psychologically walk up to and past these inner disturbances, you'll become increasingly aware that these task-resistant thoughts and feelings are just big fakes!

YOUR HIGHER DESTINY

You must prove to yourself that these thoughts and feelings are fakes in order to know the powers that come with such a discovery. Following is a glimpse of what you'll learn each time you take that step you're sure you can't.

Those negative states that try to stop you from taking the next step of any chosen journey are just psychological *special effects*. These obstacles of psychic flash-and-smoke are generated by the mind to keep you from disturbing *its* established levels of comfort. But special effects, regardless of the kind of "screen" upon which they're projected, have no reality outside of your temporary belief in their appearance.

The truth is that these inner-barriers are without real substance, and so *must* vanish the moment you pass through them. Which brings us to a great Spiritual Truth: *On the other side of the resistance is the flow.* This means that each time you call on this exercise to walk through some pocket of inner resistance, you'll find, on its other side, all the fresh energy and intelligence you'll need to go through and complete your task.

All these years you've been taught to believe that before you can hope to succeed at something, you have to first *feel* as though you can. No! To succeed you need only understand how failure is created, and then consciously refuse to cooperate with what has been defeating you from within.

SPECIAL SUMMARY

Each step *into* what you think you can't do is one step *further away* from that nature which wants you to think that circles actually go somewhere.

Every noble work is at first impossible.
       —Thomas Carlyle

EXERCISE 7

BREAK OUT OF THE BLAME GAME

SPECIAL INSIGHT

Blaming conflict-filled feelings on any condition or person outside yourself is like getting angry at your shoes for being laced too tight.

THE ROAD BEFORE YOU

Most men and women recognize the need for a healthy balanced diet because good eating habits nourish the body. Good nutrition helps keep us agile and strong. And we also like to learn new skills to expand our interests. Challenging mental activities stimulate, sharpen, and strengthen the mind.

Now here's an effective inner-life exercise designed to help you grow and develop greater Spiritual Strength: No matter what happens, *never blame anyone*—or anything— for the way *you* feel. Rising above the blame game is the same as learning how to be in total command of yourself.

Now comes an interesting surprise. In the exercise described below, it isn't what you *do* that contributes to your Spiritual Strength; it's what you *don't* do that bestows the greatest gain. And, as you'll learn, it's your aim not to blame that finally bestows the new strength you seek.

This approach to enhancing inner strength through quiet self-negation may seem confusing at first, so before we begin the hands-on part of this exercise, let's clear up any lingering questions you may have on the subject.

What is Spiritual Strength?

Spiritual Strength is many things that arise out of One. For the time being, following are three correct answers (the last one best serves our study together):

1. Spiritual Strength is the power to live spontaneously free while remaining alert and fully responsible to the need of the present moment.

2. Spiritual Strength is the courage to live exactly as you choose without the fear of being left out or of being left alone.

3. Spiritual Strength is the Higher Understanding that gives you the power *to not* act from spiritual weakness.

What is spiritual weakness?

Spiritual weakness is any unconscious aspect of your nature that either causes you—or others—to suffer. It is also anything that interferes with your development of Spiritual Strength.

What's the connection between blaming others for the way I feel and spiritual weakness?

Irritated inner states never seek solutions; they only seek reasons for why they have a right to exist! These states constantly feed you "good reasons" as to why you feel badly. The weakness that blames others blinds you to your real inner condition; which is going nowhere except around and down.

CHOOSING YOUR NEW DIRECTION

The next time you feel yourself starting to become frustrated, angry, or scared, do your best to confirm this next vital insight: *Negative emotions cannot exist without having something to blame for their punishing presence.*

The clearer for yourself you can make this spiritual fact—about the dualistic nature of spiritual weakness—the better prepared you'll be to take your next step toward higher Spiritual Strength. Your discovery leads you to this totally new action. Whatever it takes, don't express that surfacing irritation by naming or blaming anything outside of yourself as being its cause.

Even if you have to remove yourself physically from the developing situation, then do it. Find some way to temporarily isolate yourself—*along with* your smoldering emotional state. Please note: Isolate yourself along with your agitation.

YOUR HIGHER DESTINY

If it helps to make what appears to be a bitter pill taste better, think of these inner-trials as The Pause That Spiritually Strengthens, for a New Strength is exactly what you'll win for yourself each time you elect to work with this exercise. The powerful principles behind your coming success are further illuminated in the following paragraph.

Voluntarily isolating yourself along with your irritated thoughts and feelings doesn't mean cutting them off; nor does it mean that you should pretend that you're not on fire. Suppression of these weak inner states is just the opposite of angrily expressing them, and every bit as harmful. Don't express—or suppress—any negative state. Besides, either one of these opposite approaches always produces the same results: *Nothing changes* except for what's *being blamed*. Choosing to *not blame* lifts you above both of these losing choices.

Your conscious non-action turns you into the objective witness of your own superheated emotions. And from the safety of this Higher awareness you see about yourself what you couldn't see before because of all the inner fire and smoke. Your discoveries empower you to cancel the real cause of your inner combustibility. Not only is your self-command restored, but it's heightened. Each discovery of an unseen weakness heralds the coming of a greater Spiritual Strength.

Be sure to Practice The Pause That Spiritually Strengthens. Refuse to blame.

SPECIAL SUMMARY

Choose to change right now, and you won't have to worry about how to be different next time.

> *The strength of a man sinks in the hour of trial: But there doth live a power that to the battle girdeth the weak.*
>
> —*Joanna Baillie*

Exercise 8

ERASE THOSE FEARFUL FEELINGS

SPECIAL INSIGHT

There is no such thing as a shaky situation, so any time you start to tremble, don't look around you for the fault. Look inward. It is the inner ground you are standing on that is not solid.

THE ROAD BEFORE YOU

That seemingly scary condition, whatever it may be, is not the problem. It's your reaction that has you shaking. And that's why, if you'll become conscious of a fearful condition instead of afraid of it, you'll change forever your relationship with fear. It's true.

Being conscious of your fear empowers you to interact with it in an entirely new way. This new inner relationship gives you the power to be awake to your fear's scary influences, instead of being their unconscious slave. And as each day you discover something new about the shaky nature of your own fearful reactions, those reactions lose their power over you. Why? You see them for what they have always been: unintelligent mechanical forces.

To be consciously afraid means that *you know* you are frightened, but at the same time, to know that these very fears, as real as they may seem, *are not you.*

Fear is really nothing other than a self-limiting reaction that we've always mistaken for a shield of self-protection. It's time to let it go, which you can do anytime you want. Here's how: *Dare to proceed, even while being afraid.*

Employing this simple but higher instruction to proceed even while being afraid will not only show you the strange faces of all those habitual reactions that have had you on the run, but it will also empower you to start seeing through them. And, as you'll gratefully discover, each of your new insights into their actual nature removes some of their power over you. Better yet, their loss is your gain! The following exercise will help you face those fearful feelings and erase them from your life once and for all.

CHOOSING YOUR NEW DIRECTION

Do you know someone whom you would rather run from than run into? Most of us do! Nevertheless, starting right Now, resolve never again to avoid any person who scares you. In fact, whether at home or work, go ahead and walk right up to that critical or aggressive person and say exactly what you want, instead of letting the fear tell you to do what it wants. Have no ideas at all about the way things should or shouldn't go. Of course, this exercise is not an excuse to be cruel or rude.

Remember, your aim in working with this exercise in self-liberation is not to win an ego victory, but rather to watch and learn something new about yourself. Drop any other misplaced self-conscious concerns. Let that person see you shake, if that's what starts to happen. What do you care? It's only temporary. Besides, that unpleasant person before you can't know it, but you're shaking yourself awake!

Stand your inner ground even if it feels as though you might fall through the floor. Allow your reactions to roll by you—instead of letting them carry you away as they've always done in the past.

Your Higher Destiny

If you'll fight for yourself in this new way, it won't be the floor beneath you that you feel open. *It will be your inner eyes!* And what they see is that this flood—of what were once unconscious reactions—has its own life story; a shaky story that up until now you'd taken as your own. But it's not. You see these fears don't belong to you, and that they never have. Everything about your life changes in this one moment. Here's what has been revealed to you:

You've never been afraid of another person. The only thing you've ever been frightened by is your own thoughts about that person. Yes, you did feel fear, but it wasn't yours. And it wasn't toward someone stronger than you. The fear you always felt was in what you *thought* he or she was thinking about you. Amazing isn't it? You have been afraid of your own thoughts.[1]

Facing your fearful feelings brings them to an end because if you proceed while being afraid, you'll see all that has been scaring you...is you.

[1]From *The Secret of Letting Go* by Guy Finley (Llewellyn Publications, 1994).

SPECIAL SUMMARY

You only have to enter the fear of the unknown once, while you must live the fear of *pretending you know* with each pretense.

> *There is great beauty in going through life without anxiety or fear. Half our fears are baseless, and the other half discreditable.*
>
> —*Christian Bovee*

Exercise 9

RELEASE AND RELAX YOURSELF

SPECIAL INSIGHT

Natural and unrestricted energy is to your health, happiness, and spiritual development as a snow-fed river is to a high mountain lake; both must be renewed each day.

THE ROAD BEFORE YOU

Most people spend much of their lives in a constant struggle to hold themselves together. Even a brief glance shows us that a life spent in this futile fashion is most likely an unproductive one. The energies that are meant to be poured into creative expression and continued self-development are used instead to just keep common things in place. The following special exercise, one of my favorites, is all about *letting yourself fall apart.*

Please! Don't be put off by the mere mention of this unusual approach to physical and spiritual revitalization. Once you release the energies you have wasted in undetected physical tension, you can redirect them to supply you with an abundant source of inner peace, higher intuition, and an unshakable sense of well-being.

There really is a secret way to let yourself go that will, at the same time, get you going—and doing—and feeling better than you have in a long time. Read on!

Each day we are allotted a certain amount of life-energy. In the East this inner force is called *chi*; in India, *prana.* The name of these energies varies by culture, but not the fact of its existence. If you doubt this daily distribution of life-force, ask yourself the following three questions, and then seriously ponder their answers.

1. Where does the energy come from that's allowing you to hold this book—or to have the thoughts and feelings you're experiencing right now?

2. Are you the source of the life-force that beats your heart and empowers you to take that breath you just took?

3. Are you the creator of your own animating energy, or are you *its* creation?

These answers should be clear.

The energy used to sustain our lives is given to us daily. But how those energies are used is given to us to decide. So this exercise is about making the conscious decision to Relax and Release Yourself.

With conscious effort, you can learn to release those vital energies that are being wasted in undetected physical tension. What will liberating these natural forces do for you? Everything!

Imagine what happens to a flourishing orchard when the stream that naturally irrigates it is accidentally blocked or diverted by a large, fallen boulder. The orchard is able to continue living, but not nearly to its potential. Growth is stunted; life held back.

Now imagine that obstructing rock being removed. The waters return and with them the orchard's original vitality. New, vigorous growth is ensured.

Common physical tension is a boulder that blocks—and wastes—our overall energies. Poor health, irritated nerves, and vague anxieties are just a few of the ways blocked energies negatively impact our everyday lives.

CHOOSING YOUR NEW DIRECTION

The following is a soothing and sound way to remove invisible inner rocks and realize refreshing new vitality. At least three times a day, decide to relax and release yourself. Use the technique that follows, but don't get tensed up trying to comply with a set of instructions.

Close your eyes and bring your attention to the top of your head. Become aware of your scalp area and those muscles that span across your forehead and temples. Allow them to relax. Give these muscles a quiet mental command to let go, and then let them do as you've asked. If necessary (and most likely it will be), repeat this silent release instruction and letting-go action several times until you feel a definite response. Don't get frustrated if at first you don't succeed. Your muscles have probably been tense for so long they may not know how to relax, let alone remain at ease in that state. Stick with it.

In a few moments, or however long it may take, when your muscles yield to your decision to relax, you'll feel a pleasant sensation ease down from the crown of your head and continue to move downward along its sides. Give your complete attention to the inviting movement of this spreading relaxation. Let yourself go with its gentle flow.

Now, while remaining aware of the forces you've set in motion, take the next step. Place your attention on the muscles all around—and particularly just beneath—your eyes.

There's a tremendous amount of tension stored in this facial muscle group. In fact, these muscles may be so rigid that, at first mental survey, this whole area may feel as though it's locked up, and unable to be released. Be patient with yourself, but persist. This stubborn tension will yield.

As these energies are released, you may feel some trembling or quivering in those areas; have no concern. In time, as you continue to refine this exercise and keep these muscles relaxed all day long, you'll feel your entire facial structure start to change. There's a good chance your eyesight could improve. Who knows? You might even get better looking!

Continue to relax and release yourself by applying the same procedures to the area around your mouth. Stay in conscious touch with yourself to see that all previously released muscle groups are remaining at ease. Now go ahead and relax the neck, shoulders, chest, arms and hands. Use the same technique of focusing on a body part or muscle group and consciously deciding to relax that part of yourself.

If you want to, and if time permits, relax and release yourself in this way all the way down to your toes. If you have trouble falling asleep at night, this complete body release is especially helpful for inducing a deep relaxed state. You'll awaken more refreshed too.

YOUR HIGHER DESTINY

Remember: Freedom is natural. While on the road to self-release, allow your natural interest and the inner discoveries it reveals to be your final guide.

When you first begin to practice this exercise, find a comfortable place where you can be alone. Before too long, however, you'll learn to apply this energy-releasing and life-renewing inner technique anywhere, anytime, and under any circumstances.

Eventually, after you get the feel for it, you'll be able to do this exercise with your eyes open.

It's always the right time to be relaxed. Create your own abbreviated form of these self-release techniques. Learn to release and relax yourself while you're on the phone, watching TV, or even when you're out dining with friends.

SPECIAL SUMMARY

Every day: casual, but industrious. Every moment: relaxed, but alert.

If the mind, that rules the body, ever so far forgets itself as to trample on its slave, the slave is never generous enough to forgive the injury, but will rise and smite the oppressor.

—Henry Wadsworth Longfellow

Exercise 10

STOP THIS SECRET
SELF-SABOTAGE

SPECIAL INSIGHT
There is no pleasing the fear that you may displease others.

THE ROAD BEFORE YOU
It's a little-known yet much denied fact that people treat you the way you secretly ask to be treated. Your unspoken request that determines how others behave toward you is extended to—and received by—everyone you meet. This petition is broadcast, second by second, in the form of silent messages emanating from your own invisible inner life.

What is your invisible inner life? It's the way you actually feel—as opposed to the way you're trying to appear—when meeting any person or event.

In other words, your invisible inner life is your real inner condition. It's this state of internal affairs that communicates with others long before any words are exchanged. These silent signals from your inner self are what a person receives first upon meeting you. The reading of them determines, from that point forward, the basis of your relationship. This unseen dialogue that goes on behind the scenes whenever two or more people meet is commonly understood as "sizing one another up." But here's the point of this introduction.

We're often led to act against ourselves by an undetected weakness that goes before us— trying to pass itself off to others—as a strength. This is secret *self-sabotage*. It sinks us in our personal and business relationships as surely as a torpedo wrecks the ship it strikes. Learning how to stop this self-sinking is the focus of this exercise. Let's begin by gathering the higher insights we'll need to succeed.

Any person you feel the need to control or dominate—so that he or she will treat you as you "think" you should be treated—will always be in charge of you...and treat you accordingly. Why? Because anyone from whom you want something, psychologically speaking, is always in secret command of you. The dynamics of this spiritual law are revealed in the following paragraph.

It would never dawn on any person to want to be more powerful or superior to someone else unless there was some psychic character within him or her that secretly felt itself to be weaker or lesser than that other individual. From where else would such a petty concern originate if not out of an unseen, unsettling feeling of inferiority?

Genuine inner strength neither competes nor compares itself to others any more than an eagle wants to fly like a crow or waddle like a duck. Neither real strength nor regal eagle has any need to prove anything.

What this important lesson teaches us is that any action we take to *appear* strong before another person is actually read by that person as a weakness. If you doubt this finding, review the past interactions and results of your own relationships. The general rule of thumb is that the more you demand or crave the respect of others the less likely you are to receive it. If you've ever tried to raise children, you know this is true.

So it makes no sense to try and change the way others treat you by learning calculated behaviors or attitude techniques in order to appear in charge. The only thing these clever cover-ups really produce is yet another source of secret inner conflict; which, in turn, only fuels further self-sabotage. Besides, what you're really looking for in your relationships isn't command over others—*but over yourself.* So what's the answer?

CHOOSING YOUR NEW DIRECTION

Stop *trying* to be strong. Instead, start catching yourself about to act from weakness.

Don't be too surprised by this unusual instruction. A brief examination reveals its wisdom. Following are ten examples of where you may be secretly sabotaging yourself while wrongly assuming you're strengthening your position with others.

1. Fawning before people to win their favor.

2. Expressing contrived concern for someone's well-being.

3. Making small talk to smooth out the rough edges.

4. Hanging onto someone's every word.

5. Looking for someone's approval.

6. Asking if someone is angry with you.

7. Fishing for a kind word.

8. Trying to impress someone.

9. Gossiping.

10. Explaining yourself to others.

Let's look at this last act of secret self-sabotage, explaining yourself to others, and use it to see how we can transform what has always been the seed of some self-sinking act into a conscious source of self-command.

The next time you feel as though you need to explain yourself to someone (other than to your employer as it may concern his or her business affairs), give yourself a quick and simple internal test. This test will help you check for and cancel any undetected weakness that's about to make you sabotage yourself.

Here's what to do: *Run a pressure check.*

Here's how:

Come wide awake and run a quick inner scan within yourself to see if that question you're about to answer—or that answer you're about to give, without having been asked for it—is something *you* really want to do. Or are you about to explain yourself because you're afraid of some as yet undisclosed consequence if you don't?

Your Higher Destiny

This self-administered test for inner pressure is how you tell if your forthcoming explanation is truly voluntary, or if you're on the verge of being shanghaied into an unconscious act of self-sabotage. Your awareness of any pressure building within you is proof that it's some form of fear—and not you—that wants to do the explaining, fawning, impressing, blabbing, or whatever the self-sabotaging act the inner pressure is pushing you to commit.

Each time you feel this pressurized urge to give yourself away, silently but solidly refuse to release this pressure by giving in to its demands. It may help you to succeed sooner if you know that *fear has no voice unless it tricks you into giving it one.* So stay silent. Your conscious silence stops self-sabotage.

SPECIAL SUMMARY

In any and every given moment of your life, you are either in command of yourself...or you are being commanded.

> *In all our weaknesses we have one ele-*
> *ment of strength if we recognize it. Here,*
> *as in other things, knowledge of danger*
> *is often the best means of safety.*
>
> —*E. P. Roe*

Exercise 11

GO QUIET

SPECIAL INSIGHT

The frantic search for any answer only delivers answers on the same frantic level.

THE ROAD BEFORE YOU

One of the most powerful forces in the universe available to human beings is also one of the least understood and appreciated. The subject of this exercise is *Silence*.

The wise words of Richard Cecil, an eighteenth-century English author and theologian, set the stage for our study and invite us to begin:

The grandest operations, both in nature and Grace, are the most silent and imperceptible. The shallow brook babbles in its passage and is heard by everyone; but the coming of the seasons is silent and unseen. The storm rages and alarms, but its fury is soon exhausted, and its effects are but partial and soon remedied; but the dew, though gentle and unheard, is immense in quantity, and is the very life of large portions of the earth. And these are pictures of the operations of Grace in the church and in the soul.

But don't be mislead. Reach no conclusions about the true nature of what is quiet. The secret strength of silence can be as practical in your everyday life as is its real character to be life changing. You can actually have—and benefit directly from—a quiet mind.

To help bring this important and higher self-possibility down to earth, I've prepared a list of twenty-five powers that can be directly attributed to a mind that has found real silence. Be amazed! And then take action. The exercise that follows this list places you on the inner road that leads to the source of these true strengths.

A Quiet Mind:

1. Is spontaneously creative in any situation.

2. Can neither betray itself nor anyone else.

3. Rests naturally when it isn't naturally active.

4. Knows without thinking.

5. Seeks nothing outside of itself for strength.

6. Detects and easily rejects psychic intruders.

7. Never compromises itself.

8. Can't be flattered or tempted.

9. Doesn't waste valuable energy.

10. Fears nothing.

11. Can't outsmart itself.

12. Is never the victim of its own momentum.

13. Refreshes itself.

14. Is in relationship with a Higher Intelligence.

15. Never struggles with painful thoughts.

16. Is instantly intuitive.

17. Gives its undivided attention to its tasks.

18. Receives perfect direction from within.

19. Deeply enjoys the delight of its own quietness.

20. Lives above expectations and disappointments.

21. Can't be captured by regrets.

22. Commands every event it meets.

23. Lives in a state of Grace.

24. Never feels lonely.

25. Knows and helps quietly design its
    own destiny.

When you want to directly enjoy the sunshine, you must go outdoors. You understand you have to take yourself physically to a place where the warming rays of the sun can fall upon you without interference. Likewise, when you want to know the powers that circulate through a quiet mind, you must take yourself to that place where this Silent Strength can make itself known to you. To go quiet, you must go within.

In those days now past, when Christ told his disciples to seek the Kingdom of Heaven within, his words of Wisdom were not the religion they've become today. They were alive with secret but ever-so-practical instructions on how a person could discover and realize a secret part of himself or herself that was not a part of what was then—and of what still remains—a conflict-torn and weary world.

This Master Instruction still holds true. If we want to know that stillness, that silent strength, a peace that passes all understanding, *we must go within*. We must *go quiet*.

CHOOSING YOUR NEW DIRECTION

The best time to practice going quiet is when the world around you is already in a natural state of silence. Early morning, upon arising, and just before you go to sleep are the most likely times to yield the best results. But as you'll no doubt come to discover for yourself, *anytime* is the right time to go quiet.

Find a place to sit, such as a comfortable chair, where your back can be supported and held straight. Let your hands rest, open or closed, in any position that won't cause tension to themselves, your arms, or shoulders. Remain seated for the duration of your practice. Twenty to thirty minutes twice a day is a suggested minimum time to sit quietly. But do the best you can. There are no laws that govern inner silence. Besides, the day may come when you'd like to sit for longer durations, so you be the judge. Let the length of this time for inner quiet be whatever it wants to be.

Allow your legs to assume whatever position is most naturally relaxed for them. It's better if you don't cross your legs one over the other as this posture interferes with your circulation and the ensuing discomfort will become a distraction.

Once your body is situated and in relative ease, close your eyes and let your awareness sweep over the whole of your body. (To enhance the benefits of this exercise, use the practices found in Exercise 9, "Release and Relax Yourself.") Adjust your limbs again, if necessary, so that no individual part of your physical self is calling out for your attention.

Now, with your eyes still gently closed, let your shoulders take the full weight of your head. You should actually be able to feel the physical transfer of this weight take place.

Then give the weight of your shoulders and your arms to the armrests of your chair, or to whatever part of your body is beneath them. If you're doing this properly, you'll be surprised how much of your own bodily weight you were unnecessarily supporting without knowing it!

Finally, give all this collective weight—head, shoulders, arms, upper body, buttocks, and legs—to the chair or sofa you're sitting upon. Consciously transfer the weight. Let it go. Then let yourself sink into the feeling that comes with releasing all this unconscious physical stress and tension.

The next step is to continue expanding this relaxed and increased awareness of your body to include within it the awareness of your thoughts and feelings. In other words, bring into your enhanced physical awareness the further awareness of what your mind and emotions are doing in the moment. *You* watch *yourself.*

YOUR HIGHER DESTINY

This form of self-observation is as interesting as it is challenging. To ensure your success in this going within and going quiet, consider yourself as being a naturalist of the mind.

A good wildlife naturalist casually observes the diverse ways of birds or bunnies without interfering. In order to study and learn, he or she just watches. And that's what you must learn to do as you journey within. You're to be an impartial witness to the life of your own thoughts and feelings. Let them fly and hop around within you without the slightest concern for their direction or character. Neither resist nor let yourself be drawn into any of their attention-stealing antics.

Again, all you want to do is watch. Detached self-observation is your aim. Each time you realize that you're no longer watching, but rather that you've been captured by a thought or feeling and are being carried along by it, just quietly withdraw yourself from that temporary psychic wave. Come back to the awareness of yourself in the Present Moment.

This part of your practice is the heart and soul of going—and knowing—quiet. You must experience it for yourself. As you sit, let go, give up, go within, and watch. And over and over again, bring your awareness of yourself back into the awareness of the Present Moment.

One special way to help "ground" yourself in the Now is to use your awareness of each out-breath as a reminder to give all your weight back to the chair. Each time you breathe out, let yourself go completely. Stay watchful and consciously drop the heaviness of your body, mind, and emotions. Let something else be responsible for their weight. This is the greatest feeling in the world, *and* it prepares you for the eventual Higher stages of this exercise.

Pay no attention to what your own thoughts and feelings are trying to tell you the whole time you're sitting. Which is namely this: "You should give up this worthless, unproductive practice!"

Learn to watch *and drop* these dark inner voices. They don't want you to succeed and there's a good reason why: They can't dwell in that silent world you wish to enter and that wishes to enter you.

So persist! You will prevail. For even as you struggle to stay aware of yourself in the Present Moment, that moment itself changes. And as it does, so do you.

Slowly, subtly at first, but eventually even beyond your mind's protests, the distinction between your sense of self and your awareness of the Present Moment melts away. And as it does, a new, deeper sense of silence floods into you; filling your awareness with itself and, at the same time, with yet another Awareness that the source of this supreme stillness *is arising out of your own Being.* It washes everything out of its way. And so arrives a quiet mind.

SPECIAL SUMMARY

Just as you can see farther on a clear day, new
understanding flowers in a quiet mind.

*The sovereignty of nature has been allot-
ted to the silent forces. The moon makes
not the faintest echo of a noise, yet it
draws millions of tons of tidal waters to
and fro at its biding. We do not hear the
sun rise, nor the planets set. So, too, the
dawning of the greatest moment in a
man's life comes quietly, with none to
herald it to the world. In that Stillness
alone is born the knowledge of the
Overself. The gliding of the mind's boat
into the lagoon of the spirit is the gen-
tlest thing I know; it is more hushed
than the fall of eventide.*

—Dr. Paul Brunton

PART THREE

SUCCESS THROUGH HIGHER SELF-STUDIES

Set Your Sights on
Self-Liberation

The eleven inner life exercises described in this book share one life-changing objective: They are all about awakening you to new and Higher levels of yourself through increased self-awareness. But as you proceed with your studies and practices, please keep this one, very important, fact before your inquiring mind: There is no scale, no measuring stick for this new inner awareness. You cannot measure it any more than you can measure the cosmos.

What this means is that in our inner work to awaken and realize ourselves, we must begin where we begin, and put away any other concerns about where that beginning is.

It's enough just to make a start, wherever that may be. What difference does it make at what point you enter into a great river? Sooner or later, all its waters reach and pour into the sea.

Never let discouragement have the final word and one day there will be nothing left to discuss. Besides, you can have just as many new beginnings as you're willing to leave behind all your ideas about yourself. Nothing in this world, or in any other, can stop you from discovering your Original, Free Being. This has always been your destiny, as Walt Whitman confirms:

> *The central urge in every atom [is] to return to its divine source and origin.*

As a final review and summary of the important lessons in this book, following are ten secret ways higher self-studies can help you succeed in life.

1. Higher self-studies reveal that your nature is your fortune, so better luck begins with a change of self.

2. Higher self-studies hold many benefits for the sincere student, like the deep-sea diver who discovers a treasure chest lying buried beneath a bed of pearls.

3. Higher self-studies introduce your mind to a Higher Body of Wisdom whose elevated Nature lifts you, as wind does the wings of an eagle.

4. Higher self-studies prove that permitting your life direction to be determined by the way the world turns is like using the pointer of a wind-lashed weather vane for your compass and guide.

5. Higher self-studies prove that changing the way you see your life changes the life you see.

6. Higher self-studies pave the happy and relief-filled way to a new life that isn't governed by ceaseless compromise and painful self-interest.

7. Higher self-studies reveal secret sources of conflict, as in discovering that the chief thief responsible for stealing your peace of mind *is your own certainty that you already know* the real nature of security.

8. Higher self-studies provide superior self-safety by helping you develop a new awareness that can see through highly reflective surfaces, such as well-polished personalities that conceal hidden motives.

9. Higher self-studies teach you the Wisdom of letting go, which has nothing to do with giving up on your life— or into self-defeating desires.

10. Higher self-studies make it clear that looking for a sense of self-permanence in the way others think about you is like trying to make a plaster cast of the wind.

A SPECIAL NOTE
TO THE READER

To receive your free encouraging poster of helpful inner-life insights as well as information on Guy Finley's books, tapes, and ongoing classes, write to:

The Life of Learning Foundation
PO Box 170D
Merlin, Oregon 97532

To receive your free copy of *30 Keys to Change Your Destiny*, a powerful pocketbook version of the inner-life exercises in *Designing Your Own Destiny*, plus nineteen more fascinating self-discoveries, send a self-addressed stamped envelope along with $1 (Outside U.S.A., $3 U.S. funds) to:

Life of Learning
PO Box 170DB
Merlin, Oregon, 97532

If you enjoyed the self-liberating material in *Designing Your Own Destiny*, you won't want to miss reading Guy Finley's book *Freedom from the Ties that Bind* (Llewellyn, 1994).

Help spread the Light! If you know of someone who is interested in these Higher Ideas, please send his or her name and address to The Life of Learning Foundation at the above address. The latest complete list of Guy Finley's books, booklets, and tapes will be sent to them. Thank you!

On the following pages you will find listed, with their current prices, some of the books now available on related subjects. Your book dealer stocks most of these and will stock new titles in the Llewellyn series as they become available. We urge your patronage.

TO GET A FREE CATALOG

To obtain our full catalog, you are invited to write (see address below) for our bi-monthly news magazine/catalog, *Llewellyn's New Worlds of Mind and Spirit*. A sample copy is free, and it will continue coming to you at no cost as long as you are an active mail customer. Or you may subscribe for just $10 in the United States and Canada ($20 overseas, first class mail). Many bookstores also have *New Worlds* available to their customers. Ask for it.

TO ORDER BOOKS AND TAPES

If your book store does not carry the titles described on the following pages, you may order them directly from Llewellyn by sending the full price in U.S. funds, plus postage and handling (see below).

Credit card orders: VISA, MasterCard, American Express are accepted. Call us toll-free within the United States and Canada at 1-800-THE-MOON.

Postage and Handling: Include $4 postage and handling for orders $15 and under; $5 for orders *over* $15. There are no postage and handling charges for orders over $100. Postage and handling rates are subject to change. We ship UPS whenever possible within the continental U.S.; delivery is guaranteed. Please provide your street address as UPS does not deliver to P.O. boxes. Orders shipped to Alaska, Hawaii, Canada, Mexico and Puerto Rico will be sent via first class mail. Allow 4-6 weeks for delivery. **International orders:** Airmail – add retail price of each book and $5 for each non-book item (audiotapes, etc.); Surface mail – add $1 per item. **Minnesota residents add 7% sales tax.**

Llewellyn Worldwide
P.O. Box 64383-791, St. Paul, MN 55164-0383, U.S.A.
For customer service, call (612) 291-1970.

THE SECRET OF LETTING GO
by Guy Finley
Whether you need to let go of a painful heartache, a destructive habit, a frightening worry or a nagging discontent, *The Secret of Letting Go* shows you how to call upon your own hidden powers and how they can take you through and beyond any challenge or problem. This book reveals the secret source of a brand-new kind of inner strength.

In the light of your new and higher self-understanding, emotional difficulties such as loneliness, fear, anxiety and frustration fade into nothingness as you happily discover they never really existed in the first place.

With a foreword by Desi Arnaz Jr., and introduction by Dr. Jesse Freeland, *The Secret of Letting Go* is a pleasing balance of questions and answers, illustrative examples, and stimulating dialogues that allow the reader to share in the exciting discoveries that lead up to lasting self-liberation.

This is a book for the discriminating, intelligent, and sensitive reader who is looking for *real* answers.
0-87542-223-3, 240 pgs., 5 1/4 x 8, softcover
$9.95

THE SECRET WAY OF WONDER
Insights from the Silence
by Guy Finley
Introduction by Desi Arnaz, Jr.

Discover an inner world of wisdom and make miracles happen! Here is a simple yet deeply effective system of illuminating and eliminating the problems of inner mental and emotional life.

The Secret Way of Wonder is an interactive spiritual workbook, offering guided practice for self-study. It is about Awakening the Power of Wonder in yourself. A series of 60 "Wonders" (meditations on a variety of subjects: "The Wonder of Change," "The Wonder of Attachments," etc.) will stir you in an indescribable manner. This is a bold and bright new kind of book that gently leads us on a journey of Spiritual Alchemy where the journey itself is the destination ... and the destination is our need to be spiritually whole men and women.

Most of all, you will find out through self investigation that we live in a friendly, intelligent and living universe that we can reach into and that can reach us.

0-87542-221-7, 192 pgs., 5 1/4 x 8, softcover

$9.95

FREEDOM FROM THE TIES THAT BIND
The Secret of Self Liberation
by Guy Finley

Imagine how your life would flow *without* the weight of those weary inner voices constantly convincing you that "you can't," or complaining that someone else should be blamed for the way *you* feel. The weight of the world on your shoulders would be replaced by a bright, new sense of freedom. Fresh, new energies would flow. *You could choose to live the way* YOU *want.* In *Freedom from the Ties that Bind,* Guy Finley reveals hundreds of Celestial, but down-to-earth, secrets of Self-Liberation that show you exactly how to be fully independent, and *free of any condition not to your liking.* Even the most difficult people won't be able to turn your head or test your temper. Enjoy solid, meaningful relationships founded *in conscious choice*—not *through self-defeating compromise.* Learn the secrets of unlocking the door to your own Free Mind. Be empowered to break free of any self-punishing pattern, and make the discovery that who you really are is already everything you've ever wanted to be.

0-87542-217-9, 240 pgs., 6 x 9, softcover

$10.00

COMO TRIUNFAR SOBRE LA ANSIEDAD Y LOS PROBLEMAS

by Guy Finley
Prólogo por Desi Arnaz, Jr.
Introducción por Dr. Jesse Freeland
Especial mensaje de Vernon Howard
Traducción por Daisy M. Morales, B.A.

Unbest-seller fácilmente logrado cuando la edición en el lenguaje inglés fue publicada en 1990, este libro ofrece variados conocimientos de la vida en como soltar su propia fuerza interior y vivir la vida según sus propios términos.

Desi Arnaz, Jr. dice, "Las curativas realidades presentadas en este libro me han rescatado de más persecuciones y hábitos de derrota-propia que lo que cuido de mencionar.

"Este libro está lleno con las correctas herramientas para transformar los problemas en triunfos. Guy Finley toma la Sabiduría de los Siglos y la usa para enseñar poco a poco a sus lectores curar los lugares en sus propias mentes donde problemas psicológicos se originan.

"El libro de Guy Finley es una muy poderosa y además jovial y alegre lección de aprender para dejar ir quien usted piensa que usted es."

1-56718-277-1, 5 1/4 x 8, 240 pgs. $9.95